ideals

AUTUMN

Season of mists and mellow fruitfulness!
Close bosom-friend of the maturing sun;
Conspiring with him how to load and bless
With fruit the vines that round the thatcheaves run;
To bend with apples the moss'd cottage-trees,
And fill all fruit with ripeness to the core;
To swell the gourd and plump the hazel shells
With a sweet kernel; to set budding more,
And still more, later flowers for the bees,
Until they think warm days will never cease,
For summer has o'erbrimmed their clammy cells.

John Keats

ISBN 0-8249-1054-0

IDEALS—Vol. 44, No. 6 September MCMLXXXVII IDEALS (ISSN 0019-137X) is published eight times a year, February, March, May, June, August, September, November, December by IDEALS PUBLISHING CORPORATION, Nelson Place at Elm Hill Pike, Nashville, Tenn. 37214-8000
Second class postage paid at Nashville, Tennessee, and additional mailing offices.

POSTMASTER: Send address changes to Ideals, Post Office Box 148000, Nashville, Tenn. 37214-8000

Published simultaneously in Canada.

SINGLE ISSUE—$3.50
ONE-YEAR SUBSCRIPTION—eight consecutive issues as published—$15.95
TWO-YEAR SUBSCRIPTION—sixteen consecutive issues as published—$27.95
Outside U.S.A., add $4.00 per subscription year for postage and handling.

 Printed and bound in U.S.A. by the Banta Co., Menasha, Wisconsin.

Front and back covers by Gene Ahrens

Inside front cover by Gerald Koser

Inside back cover by Ken Dequaine

Catch the Leaves Before They Fall

Catch the leaves before they fall;
Catch a glimpse of each and all.
Leaves of every vibrant hue . . .
Scarlet red, gold, orange, too.

Leaves from maple, aspen, oak,
Linden, hickory, dogwood . . . oh,
Colored leaves from all the trees
God placed here for you and me.

Catch the leaves before they fall,
That in winter, you'll recall
Colored days of myriad hues
Tucked within the heart of you.

Catch the leaves before they fall;
May each glimpse your heart enthrall.
As you watch in ecstasy,
Catch the fall before it leaves.

Loise Pinkerton Fritz

Photo Opposite
VINES ON TREE
Gene Ahrens

Beauty in the Fall

If I could only find the words
The beauty of the leaves express.
The autumn colors of the trees
In all their glory now are dressed.

No living artist e'er can paint
The vivid reds and gold of leaves.
An exquisite mosaic shawl
Is spread about the heads of trees.

A Persian carpet carefully
Is thrown across the hill and dale.
And scudding clouds of purest white
Across the wintry sky now sail.

Each season has its beauty—
The naked beauty of the tree
With winter's sparkling ice and snow—
Magnificent the scene to me.

The fragrant, pastel beauty comes
With every season of the spring.
Abundance of the earthly green
And myriad flowers she will bring.

The vivid colors summer brings
With vegetables and fruits galore.
The garden's then quite beautiful;
We could not ask for more.

Each season brings its beauty fair;
We treasure them, each one and all.
But what could be more beautiful
Than changing colors in the fall?

Gertrude Holman

NEW ENGLAND CHARM
Appel Color Photography

Rustic Painting

The mountain cabin made of logs
Clasps autumn at its gate;
Red maples turn with yellow oaks
And apples ripen late.

The fields are halloweened with hay,
Gold pumpkins on the ground;
A rail-hewn fence relaxed with years
Zigzags and curves around.

The scene is brushed from paint-glow pots,
A masterpiece of art.
I call it rustic beauty's pride
And frame it in my heart.

Inez Franck

Photo Opposite
JOHN OLIVER CABIN
Jeff Gnass

Through a Woodland

I walked through an autumn woodland
On a still October day;
The transient beauty stirred my soul
In an awe-inspiring way.

The trees attired in splendor
For autumn's gala affair,
Wore dresses of red and yellow
With a regal and festive air.

The day was clear like crystal;
The sun's rays filtered through;
The sky stretched out above me—
A matchless shade of blue.

I walked through an autumn woodland
On a still October day;
The rustle of leaves fluttering down—
The breathless hush as they settled to ground,
Is haunting my memory today.

Mary Lee Butts

Photo Opposite
FALL FOLIAGE
Fred Sieb

Editor's Note: "American Crossroads" is a regular feature of *Ideals*, presenting photographs, stories, and jokes which have been submitted by our readers, about uniquely American events or experiences. If you have a 50 to 75 word account or photograph of an unusual or interesting occurrence unique to an American lifestyle or heritage, we would like to know. Send your submission to "American Crossroads," c/o Ideals Editorial, P.O. Box 141000, Nashville, TN 37214-1000. Please send only copies of manuscripts and duplicates of photographs or slides since submissions will not be returned. We will pay $10 for each printed submission.

Today, may beautiful things happen to you, as they did to me when I found this lovely handcrafted Ojibwa birch basket filled with hand-picked wild blueberries on my doorstep. It was a gift from Ruggie Mason, a skilled Ojibway craftsman from Redby, Minnesota.

Ruggie used birch bark to fashion this basket which he sewed together with bass wood strips and sealed with pine pitch. Originally, the baskets were used by the Ojibwa to boil maple syrup, gather wild rice and fruits, and as a necessary cooking utensil.

Ruggie Mason, an American Indian, is unsurpassed in his mastery of authentic Ojibwa skills. He emphasizes the beauty of nature in his original diamond willow furniture, pipestone pipes, wooden flutes, and jewelry from stones, horns, and bones.

Constance M. Simenson
Bemidji, MN

Photos by Ken Barton

Scarecrows have been used by farmers for over 3,000 years. The figures were supposed to frighten away crop-eating birds, but the birds were not so easily fooled.

Farmers today are more apt to rely on noisemakers, such as clackers or automatic devices which sound like gunshots. However, the art of making scarecrows has not disappeared.

Near the Central California town of Vacaville, on Highway 80, the Nut Tree sponsors the Great Scarecrow contest each October. Last year, over 200 individuals and groups competed in this folk art contest for prizes of merchandise and cash; but the real winners were the thousands of people who came to see these excellent examples of American ingenuity and imagination.

Eloise Barton
Sacramento, CA

Photo Overleaf
EAST ORANGE, VERMONT
Monserrate Schwartz

Readers'

Autumn Chorus

I've whisked the leaves
From yard and hedge
And brought the hearth
wood in,
Filled the shelves with
autumn fruit,
Piled high the winter
bin.
I've bid a sad, yet fond,
farewell
To robins on the wing
And settled by the
fireside
To dream and plan for
spring!

Emily Scarlett
Cumberland, Maryland

October Thirty-First

I think the fun that children glean
From that night known as Halloween
Is less the candy and the junk
That neighbors in their bags will plunk,

But more the pleasure in the task,
The chance to hide behind a mask.
Perhaps as grown-ups, even we
Would like to change identity;

The difference is, we adults tend
To lose the joy of "let's pretend."
And that, as much as food and things,
Is what the thirty-first still brings.

Kathleen Y. Bergeron
Mojave, California

Editor's Note: Readers are invited to submit unpublished, original poetry, short anecdotes, and humorous reflections on life for possible publication in future *Ideals* issues. Please send copies only; manuscripts will not be returned. Writers will receive $10 for each published submission. Send materials to "Readers' Relfections," Ideals Publishing Corporation, Nelson Place at Elm Hill Pike, Nashville, Tennessee 37214.

Reflections

Song for Autumn

All the lovely things must go—
Hyacinths and daffodils,
Cherry blossoms white as snow,
Violets on greening hills,
Roses born of sunny June,
Hollyhock and golden-glow.
Summer passes all too soon;
All the lovely things must go.

They will vanish, so today
I must live and laugh and sing,
Garner beauty by the way,
Cherishing each perfect thing.
Then when winter brings the cold
And the cerements of snow,
I shall have some dreams to hold,
Though the lovely things must go.

Thomas Curtis Clark
Maywood, Illinois

Welcoming Autumn

We woke to discover summer was gone;
Gray chimney smoke rubbed elbows with dawn.
Nature, arrayed in a new scarlet gown,
Curtsied Miss Autumn back into town.
The leaves spread a carpet for her banquet hall;
The squirrels shared her harvest, rejoicing in fall.

Mary Borrelli
Tonawanda, New York

The Bonfire of My Youth

The bonfire glowed with a life of its own
In the beautiful fall of the year;
It fretted and crackled with gay happy sounds
In my childhood of yesteryear.

My father and I reaped a harvest of leaves,
Of crimson and brown and gold.
We gathered the mass of prunings and boughs
For the wandering flames to enfold.

The higher the flames, the higher the thrill,
The redder the glow on my cheeks;
As I shouldered the task with my wonderful dad,
Feeling safe and secure in his strength.

The tinges and hues of our autumn hill
Were keeping the flames alive,
As we poked at the fire and pondered the thought . . .
"When will the first snow arrive?"

The country air breathed of smoldering leaves
And filmy white smoke on high.
It penciled its way into the dark night
Against cold of the autumn sky.

Still glimmering through the dream of my youth
Is the fire that illumined the night
And the love that I felt with my father near
In the warmth of its firelight.

Joy Belle Burgess

Painting Opposite
AUTUMN LEAVES
John Slobodnik

Country Chronicle

The clear, crisp days of September lure me to the pastures and sidehills in search of hickory nuts. This is a ritual which began in childhood, when my family gathered to harvest the nuts. It is a ritual much like that of the squirrel and chipmunk as they gather a store of food for the coming winter.

It doesn't matter that there are competitors in the fields—squirrels who leave chompings as a sign of their visit and chipmunks with puffed-out cheeks scurrying toward stone walls. I feel like a child again as I listen to the chipmunk tremolo from the creek walls and wild grape thickets where the robins feed before flying south.

These are the days when the scarlet of the soft maples by the roadside and on the hills leaps toward the blue, cloudless sky. Fencerows are aflame with woodbine. And the sumac lights its lamps on the knoll above the barn.

On days such as these, the pungent aroma of hickory nut shucks fills the autumn air. The sound of the nuts falling from the trees can be heard in the fields. They strike tin pails with a ping and hit the ground with a thump.

Like the squirrel and chipmunk, I begin planning for those cold, sharp winter nights which lie ahead. I plan to have a store of hickory nuts in the house, cracked and ready to use in cakes and cookies, salads and fudge.

Fragments left from the cracking of the nuts will be scattered on windowsills and in feeders, providing a feast for the birds. The chickadees will come, as will the nuthatches, titmice, and woodpeckers.

Squirrels will feed on the nuts stored in the hollow trees in the woods. Chipmunks will rouse themselves long enough to feed on the nuts hidden in their dens.

I am content knowing that bird and squirrel, chipmunk and my own family will long savor the flavor gleaned from hickory nuts gathered on the bright, blue days of September.

Lansing Christman

Migration

The birds know when the snows are near
  To follow autumn's rain.
Without delay they disappear
  Till spring shall come again.

They must behold with clearer eyes
  What mortals fail to see.
For wiser than a man is wise
  They prove themselves to be.

Oft as I watch them come and go
  To start and close the year,
I wish a man could as surely know
  When danger's drawing near.

Yet man, who has so much to say
  And boasts so wise is he,
From what is best oft turns away
  And stays when he should flee.

Edgar A. Guest

Photo Opposite
HORICAN NATIONAL WILDLIFE REFUGE
Bob Coyle

Lanes of Autumn

Down the lanes of autumn,
Drifting on the breeze,
Comes an autumn lullaby
Singing to the trees.

O'er the sky at twilight
Hear the wild birds call,
Rustling in marsh grasses
'Mid the cattails tall.

'Neath the hills of splendor
Where the brook runs free,
Sailing ships of golden leaves
Race to meet the sea.

Down the lanes of autumn,
In burnished gold and mist,
October lies a-dreaming,
Awaiting winter's kiss.

Mildred L. Jarrell

Solitude

Oh, let me walk in the open field
Where purple asters bloom,
Where goldfinch perch on the
thistledown,
And bees drone a late summer tune.

Oh, let me walk where the
goldenrod
Lifts its regal head to the sun,
Where butterflies play in the field
all day,
And rabbits frolic in fun.

Oh, let me walk in the open field,
With the milkweed bursting its pod,
With the sun in my face and the wind
in my hair,
Where my soul feels a closeness to God.

Mrs. Paul E. King

Indian Summer

Oh, come and walk along with me
This Indian Summer day;
Let's view the brilliant tapestry
Of hills along the way.

A harvest bountiful awaits;
'Twas promised in the spring.
And now a crispy air prevails
And strange sensations brings.

The maple leaves are painted now
With bronze and scarlet tints;
The aspens dance there in the breeze
With brightest golden glints.

The leaves aflutter to the ground,
Or just perhaps they light
Upon the swirling, dancing brook—
They make a happy sight.

A small proud fern stands quietly,
Brushed with a frosty white;
It's now warm-sweater mornings and
Chilly, tingling nights.

The geese follow their leaders to
Their nests in southern climes.
Come walk with me into the woods . . .
It's Indian Summer time!

Georgia B. Adams

Photo Opposite
AN AUTUMN WALK
Robert Cushman Hayes

As Treasures Unfold

The warmth of a fire on a cold, frosty night;
The taste of a chestnut that's roasted just right;
Raking up leaves and laughing the while;
The sheer fun of falling into a leaf pile.

The warm, spicy smell of a fresh pumpkin pie;
The wind rustling by with a long, lonely sigh;
The trees, bright with color, that line every lane;
Excitement that comes with the first football
game.

The candy and costumes that make Halloween;
The crispy clear nights and the moon with a sheen;
The harvest of food from the garden and field;
Our Thanksgiving praise for this bountiful yield.

This season of splendor that comes every year
Brings happiness, wonder, and feelings of cheer.
I realize the beauties of living, untold,
While watching the treasures of autumn unfold.

Sherry Davis Gallisdorfer

Majestic Beauty

The warm, sweet kiss of summer
Is now a memory,
As autumn beauty nears
In all its majesty.

Treetops wear bright crowns
So lovely to behold;
Woodland fairies paint the leaves
Vivid red and gold.

The fields are heaped with harvest,
As earth prepares for rest;
The rosy sun sinks early
To its haven in the west.

Twilight fires crackle;
Smoke ribbons fill the air.
The pumpkin moon rocks gently,
Casting magic everywhere.

Grateful hearts are happy
When autumn spreads its hue;
And thankful prayers are echoed
Each time it comes anew.

LaVerne P. Larson

Photo Opposite
GOLDEN WHEAT
Bob Coyle

The Last Leaf

When the moving van pulled away that golden October afternoon, it took more than my furniture and a few trinkets. It took my security. I watched as the truck slowly rounded the corner and disappeared from sight.

I felt lost. My house stood empty, yet I didn't want to leave it. The windows stared at me like sad dark eyes. Gone were the fluffy Priscilla curtains, the tailored draperies, the saucy café ruffles. No longer did autumn breezes slip in through a raised sash to tempt me with the scents of burning leaves and ripened fruit. The house was a stranger now, and I felt I had lost a friend.

The hill behind me was strewn with red and gold leaf-offerings from the sugar maples. I walked through the leaves, kicking them high into the air, then watching as they fell, rustling, to the ground once more. Feeling suddenly childlike, I sat in a pile of leaves, mounding them around my legs and gathering them to me like memories. I recalled all the autumns I had known, each one pungent in its own way. But none, I mused, was as sad and lonely as this.

I lay back in the leaves, staring at the Wedgwood sky. Above me, the bare maple branches traced their pattern against the clear blue. Near the end of a small limb, a single leaf caught my eye. Why had it remained when all the others had long since given in to nature and gravity?

I watched the lone leaf flutter as the breezes tugged and pulled it, first one way and then another. It was long past the time for falling, yet the leaf's curled edges reached upward as if clutching for a firmer grip on the limb. It was clear this little leaf fought against leaving the only home it had ever known. I became caught up in this tiny drama. Would the wind be victorious? Or would this be the one dry leaf to cling to its tree through winter snows and remain, incongruous and comical amid spring's greenery? Suddenly, I saw myself.

Here I was, lying on my familiar hillside, wrapped in autumn leaves, refusing to go. My new home awaited. My old home locked and empty, stood before me, looking as solid and reliable as this sugar maple. I was clinging like this tattered leaf, afraid of change, of the unknown, of the unexpected.

The wind blew harder and the leaf shook, but still it remained linked by some unseen bond to its only security. I hoped the leaf would never give way, that it would not be pulled from the maple to fall, unnoticed, to the ground. But the leaf was dry, broken at the edges, wounded from its struggle. It had lost its beauty and color in its rigidity. The leaf was unique and had paid a price for this distinction. It hung onto the limb, but its life was gone.

The wind stilled and, suddenly undisturbed, the leaf gave up its fight. As if deciding all at once to leave of its own accord, the crisp, brown leaf floated to earth. I dashed to where it landed, picked it up carefully, and examined the stem with interest. One tiny fiber extended from the end. That tiny thread had held the leaf so tightly. Like regrets, I thought.

I turned to my empty house. Nothing bound me to it but myself. Snapping free of my last regrets, I finally said good-by and started to the car, carrying the leaf in my hand. In my new home, I thought, I will set it in a special place; and every time I see it, I will remember this afternoon.

Many autumns have since passed, and I am no longer afraid of changing, moving on, getting older, passing milestones, for I see them as the seasons—each one ushering me into a new phase of life, to another stage of growth. The old leaf has long since disintegrated, but I have never forgotten it. Each fall I find a crisp brown leaf to set upon my mantel, reminding me of the lesson I learned from the leaf of long ago.

Pamela Kennedy

Harvest Hymn

Once more the liberal year laughs out
O'er richer stores than gem or gold;
Once more with harvest-song and shout
Is nature's bloodless triumph told.

Oh, favors every year made new!
Oh, gifts with rain and sunshine sent!
The bounty overruns our due,
The fullness shames our discontent . . .

Who murmurs at his lot today?
Who scorns his native fruit and bloom?
Or sighs for dainties far away,
Beside the bounteous board of home?

Thank heaven, instead, that freedom's arm
Can change a rocky soil to gold,
That brave and generous lives can warm
A clime with northern ices cold.

And let these altars, wreathed with flowers
And piled with fruits, awake again
Thanksgivings for the golden hours,
The early and the latter rain!

John Greenleaf Whittier

Photo Opposite
SWEET CIDER STAND
Syd Greenberg
Cyr Color Photo

COLD
SWEET
CIDER
SWEET CIDER
HOGAN'S CIDER MILL
POTATOES
BETTER TIMES

Cider-Makin' Time

When the summertime had vanished
And the nights were getting cold,
Then 'twas time for makin' cider;
All the big fat jugs could hold.

Dad would gather up the apples,
Put them neatly in a pile;
Then he'd pour them in the hopper,
Humming softly all the while.

Afterwards he'd fill the presses,
While with eyes glued to the spout,
We in eagerness awaited
Till the cider trickled out.

We'd just crank a little harder
When we'd taste that luscious treat.
Nothing ever matched the flavor
Of that juice so fresh and sweet.

Oh, I cherish well those mem'ries;
Matters not the year or clime,
'Cause I feel a bit nostalgic
When it's cider-makin' time.

Mrs. Della Doane Mockridge

Bountiful Harvest

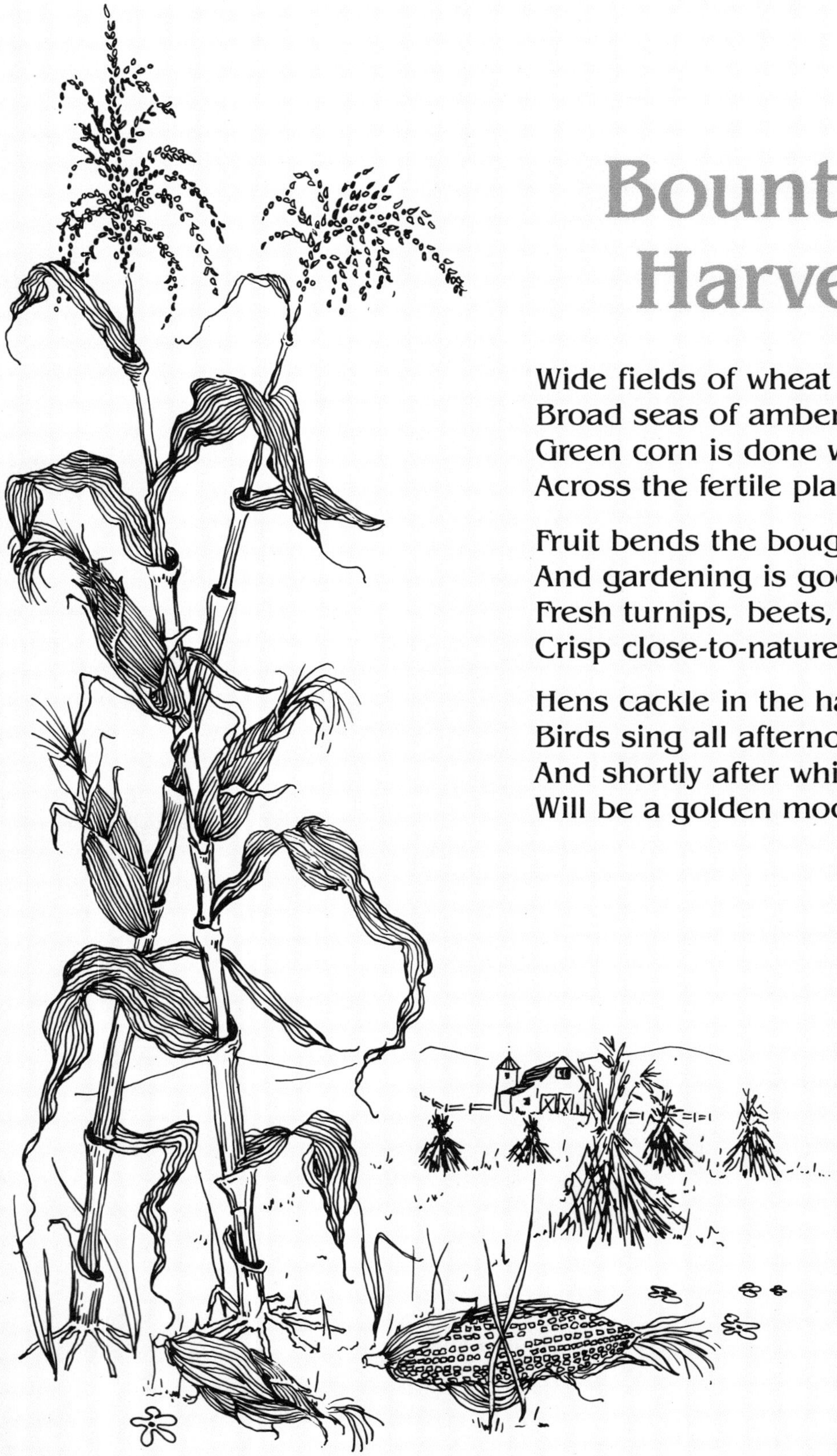

Wide fields of wheat are ripe again,
Broad seas of amber grain.
Green corn is done with plowing
Across the fertile plain.

Fruit bends the boughs of orchards low
And gardening is good—
Fresh turnips, beets, and cabbage,
Crisp close-to-nature food.

Hens cackle in the hayloft;
Birds sing all afternoon.
And shortly after whippoorwills
Will be a golden moon.

Dan A. Hoover

Photo Opposite
WHEAT COMBINE
Grant Heilman
Grant Heilman Photography

GLEANER
G

Mother's Cellar

The cellar shelves are now well stocked
With jars of every kind;
Preserves and pickles, jams and jells
Are there for you to find.

There's apple butter, thick and brown,
And apple cider, too.
It sparkles just like liquid gold,
And is waiting there for you.

There are jars of red and purple plums
And apricots of gold;
It's like a rainbow full of hues
That's ours to have and hold.

For someone dear has taken time
To put them up with care;
Her greatest joy is giving them
As gifts for folks to share.

Carice Williams

Hearty Autumn Soups

Cioppino

Makes 6 to 8 servings

- 2 1-pound cans plum tomatoes
- 1 small onion, chopped
- 1 green pepper, chopped
- 2 tablespoons chopped parsley
- 1 8-ounce can tomato sauce
- 2 cloves garlic, minced
- 2 teaspoons salt
- ¼ teaspoon pepper
- ½ teaspoon crushed oregano
- ¼ teaspoon crushed basil
- 1 10 to 12-ounce can whole clams, drained, liquid reserved
- 1 pound flounder *or* cod, cut into large pieces
- 1 pound red snapper, cut into large pieces
- ½ pound shrimp, shelled and deveined

In a stockpot, combine tomatoes, onion, green pepper, parsley, tomato sauce, garlic, salt, pepper, oregano, basil, and clam liquid; bring to a boil. Reduce heat; cover and simmer for 30 minutes. Add clams and fish; return to boiling. Reduce heat; cover and simmer for 30 minutes. Add shrimp the last 10 minutes of cooking time.

Minestrone

Makes 6 to 8 servings

- ¼ pound salt pork, diced
- 1 tablespoon olive oil
- 1 medium onion, chopped
- 1 clove garlic, minced
- 5 cups chicken stock
- 1 large can tomatoes
- 1 carrot, sliced
- 1 rib celery, chopped
- ¼ head cabbage, shredded
- 1 zucchini, sliced
- 1 1-pound can garbanzo beans, drained
- 1 1-pound can kidney beans, drained
- 1 teaspoon salt
- ½ teaspoon pepper
- 1 teaspoon oregano
- ¼ cup chopped parsley
- 1 cup macaroni
- Grated Parmesan cheese

In a stockpot, sauté salt pork until brown. Add olive oil, onion, and garlic; sauté until onion is tender. Add remaining ingredients, except macaroni and cheese. Simmer for 2 to 3 hours. Add macaroni and cook for 10 to 15 minutes, or until macaroni is tender. Garnish with Parmesan cheese. Serve with crusty bread and butter.

Split Pea Soup

Makes 8 to 10 servings

- 2 cups split peas, soaked overnight and drained
- 2 quarts water or chicken stock
- 1 ham bone *or* 2 smoked ham hocks *or* 1 smoked turkey leg or wing
- 1 medium onion, chopped
- 1 carrot, peeled and sliced
- 1 rib celery, chopped
- 1 small white potato, peeled and sliced
- ½ teaspoon thyme
- 1 bay leaf
- ¼ cup minced parsley
- 1 teaspoon salt
- ¼ cup sherry
- Sour cream

In a Dutch oven, combine all ingredients except sherry and sour cream. Bring to a boil; reduce heat and simmer for 3 to 4 hours or until peas are soft. Remove bone and bay leaf. Pour soup into food processor or blender; blend until smooth. Return to Dutch oven and heat to steaming. Add sherry and serve garnished with a dollop of sour cream.

Photo Opposite, CIOPPINO, from *Soup, Salad, Sandwich Cookbook.*

Published by Ideals Publishing Corp., Nashville, TN

Bounty of Autumn

The fields are fully ripened;
The hills shine in the sun.
With crimson, orange, and gold,
Fall of the year has come.

The haze of Indian Summer
Spreads softly o'er the land;
The wind's voice grows sharper
Because autumn is at hand.

So gather autumn's bounty,
Store apples safely away
For cheer beside the fireplace
When wintertime holds sway.

Lillie Cate Goodwin

Roadside Stand

On this glorious autumn day
We take the maple-bordered way
To the beckoning roadside stand
That flaunts the harvest of the land.

There are purple grapes, golden pears,
Red apples, and other orchard wares.
Pumpkins lie in a flaming row
And mums present a gaudy show.

Chinese lanterns are to be seen,
And cabbages, so fresh and green.
Pearly onions are for sale,
And bittersweet that edged a trail.

It's always rewarding to go
To the roadside stand where we know
That it is God who gives the yields
From the orchards, gardens, and fields.

Earle J. Grant

Photo Opposite
FALL HARVEST
Larry Lefever
Grant Heilman Photography

Kimiko's First Halloween

When evenings turn crisp and leaves change to gold, Halloween is in the air. Excitement mounts as children wiggle into favorite costumes, plan their parties, and prepare for trick-or-treating. Youngsters are wrapped in joyous preparation for a favorite American holiday. But just try to explain Halloween to a shy, Japanese woman who has recently arrived in this country.

I first met Kimiko in early October. She was a young, attractive woman who had answered my knock on her door. As the weeks passed, I found teaching English to Kimiko rewarding, a great challenge. Her dark, expressive eyes missed nothing. Laughter mingled with serious study. Because her lessons had been progressing well, I planned something extra special.

"Today, I have a surprise for you!" I announced. Pleased, Kimiko listened closely as she sat beside me. I reached down and plunked a carved pumpkin on the table, turning its face to us.

"A pumpkin with face!" Kimiko proclaimed in fascination.

"Yes, it's a jack-o'-lantern," I airily announced. The words were meaningless to Kimiko. "See, there's a candle inside, and when it's lit, the jack-o'-lantern smiles."

She watched, but her mind was elsewhere. "We eat pumpkin. We cook," she noted. To Kimiko, who had lived on a small, Japanese farm, food was too precious to use as a toy.

Had I blundered? I hesitated, but continued. "This is for Halloween," I tried to explain, pointing to the jack-o'-lantern. Kimiko listened. I produced a second pumpkin. "How would you like to draw a face on this one?"

"I try." She sounded unconvinced.

"Kimiko, you can do it," I told her. She looked at me for reassurance. Studying the jack-o'-lantern, Kimiko carefully drew her own superior design. She was an artist.

"Beautiful job! You can keep it for Halloween."

"Thank you," Kimiko timidly remarked, as she received that strange gift.

I sipped tea and proceeded. "We not only have jack-o'-lanterns on Halloween, but in just three days, children will come to your door dressed in funny clothes."

"Funny clothes?" Kimiko asked, confused.

"Yes, like a clown." She raised her eyebrows and nodded. "Like a witch," I continued, watching her closely. Kimiko didn't react. "Like Santa Claus!" I triumphantly blurted out something she might know.

Kimiko was all smiles. "Santa Claus coming?" she inquired, excited over the prospects of an early Christmas.

"Oh, no, just pretend," I assured her. No doubt this was the most confusing story Kimiko had ever heard!

Just then, her phone rang and she answered, spewing out a stream of Japanese. Was she telling a friend her teacher had gone mad?

Finally, I broke in. "Is it Suki?"

"Yes," Kimiko answered.

I took the phone, and in a few short sentences, explained what I was doing. Suki laughed. She'd been in the United States eight years and remembered her first Halloween. "I'll talk to Kimiko. She can come to my house that evening."

"Thanks, Suki, you called just in time."

"Holiday for fun?" Kimiko asked.

"Yes, just for fun," I told her. "Do you want to see what my jack-o'-lantern will look like?"

Standing beside me, Kimiko nodded. She watched me intently as I lit the small candle. The jack-o'-lantern burst alive. Kimiko clapped her hands. At a loss for words, she stamped her feet rapidly on the kitchen floor, as agile as a Spanish dancer. She'd just said a whole page! Laughter sang in the air.

Such delightful incidents were soon to end for Kimiko moved away. It's been over seven years, and seven Halloweens have passed. I can see her carving jack-o'-lanterns now, and greeting goblins at her door. Her bright smile and laughter will follow the children's raucous "trick or treat!"

I wonder if she still remembers her first Halloween? I know I'll never forget.

Gwen Whyte

To a Halloween Pumpkin

Giant golden pumpkin,
Resting in the noonday sun,
I wonder if you're dreaming
Of a magic night of fun.

Very soon you'll wear a smile
Carved by a jackknife blade,
As you glow with candlelight
While the spooks are on parade.

You'll sit proudly in the window
To view the eerie scene
As the gremlins dart by,
Celebrating Halloween.

You will radiate with beauty,
As the young and very old
Are captured in your spell
While the witching hours unfold.

Oh, giant golden pumpkin,
When Halloween is gone,
The enchantment that you weave
Will always linger on.

LaVerne P. Larson

Photo Opposite
PUMPKIN TIME
Fred Dole

Halloween

Chilling winds bite at the air,
Nipping here and snapping there.
Into swirls the world is spun,
Full of thrilling autumn fun!

Falling leaves leave tree arms bare.
Ghosts and goblins everywhere.
It's the bewitching time of year;
Spooky Halloween is here!

Bobbe Indgin

Jack-O'-Lantern Magic

My son has planned a work of art.
On just which pumpkin will he start?
This orange giant looks just right
To shape a face that is a fright.

The big, round eyes are cut with style,
Triangle nose, a wicked smile.
He lights a candle's small, brave beam
To make that jack-o'-lantern gleam.

Now which one has the brightest glow?
The boy or pumpkin, I don't know!

Louise Pugh Corder

Photo Opposite
JACK-O'-LANTERN
H. Armstrong Roberts

John
Slobodnik

Halloween Party Time

A Halloween party—
Hip-hip-hooray!
We've longed and we've waited
For this happy day.

There will be lots of games,
Pinning on donkey's tail,
And dripping wet faces
Bobbing apples from pails,

A ghost walk for certain
To frighten and scare,
With witches and goblins
Hid round everywhere.

Have you tried eating apples
From a long piece of string?
The onlookers' laughter
Will make the roof ring.

After the games
Are all over once more,
Hot chocolate and doughnuts
To eat by the score!

Ruth H. Underhill

AMUEL D. MONROE
Æ. 22.
DAVID RITTER
Æ. 47.
EWIS A. POWERS
Æ. 24.
M. F. SEVERANCE
Æ. 21.

SUMMER HOURS

It seems like only yesterday
That school let out that day;
And summer stretched, an endless dream
In which to romp and play.

It seems like only yesterday
We took our fishing poles
And dropped the first worms of the year
Into our favorite holes.

It seems like only yesterday
We swam and built a raft
And tracked each other through the wood
With Indian skill and craft.

Where have they gone, those summer hours?
They've simply flown away.
And now they're just a memory,
For school bells ring today.

Virginia Blanck Moore

WASHINGTON, NEW HAMPSHIRE
Gene Ahrens

Schooltime

What privilege it is each fall
When all our nation round,
The school bells fill the countryside
With their reverberant sound.

It is a time when freedom rings
With school bells loud and clear—
With bells of opportunity,
With bells of knowledge dear.

The eagerness is there to see,
For long before the bell,
The students chat before the doors
With summer fun to tell.

Each year excitement hits a peak
When it is early fall,
And schedules, books, and teachers, too,
Are on the tongues of all.

There's joy when school vacation comes,
And students earn a rest;
But eagerness for it to start
Is what I like the best!

Craig E. Sathoff

After School

Yes, after school on autumn days
There is so much to do,
With leaves to rake and pile high
Or just plain scamper through.

There are apples high upon the tree,
So challenging to pick,
And football games for neighbor boys—
A run, a pass, a kick!

There's garden produce to bring in
And storm windows to place,
A pumpkin that's especially large
Just waiting for a face.

There are walnuts to pick up and shell
And roses we must cover,
And long before our tasks are through,
The daylight hours are over.

For after school on autumn days
There is so much to do—
A bit of play, a bit of work,
And soon the season's through.

Craig E. Sathoff

Photo Opposite
LEAF TALK
Robert Cushman Hayes

OshKosh

Mary's Lamb

Mary Sawyer lived on a farm in Sterling, Massachusetts, during the early years of the nineteenth century. Her father adored his daughter and enjoyed taking her on long walks around their 150-acre farm. During one of these strolls—in the spring of 1814—Mary, then five, encountered the lamb which would make her famous.

There were two newborn lambs in the pen on this particular day. One was full of life, the other frail and sickly. Mary adopted the sick little lamb, bottle-fed it, and nursed it back to health. She was quite taken with the little white creature and named her pet "Snow."

That fall, Mary began classes at the Redstone School, a half-mile from the farm. Before leaving for school each day, she would visit Snow and pet him. Often, the little animal would try to follow Mary, but she always managed to close the gate before the lamb could get out.

One morning, Mary's brother Nathaniel left the gate open to see if the lamb would follow her. It did—all the way to the little red schoolhouse.

Miss Polly Kimball, the teacher, allowed the students to play with the lamb for a few minutes. Then she locked Snow in a shed at the back of the school while her students returned to their reading, writing and 'rithmetic.

Mary's classmate, John Roulstone, delighted in the lamb's antics that day. At Christmastime, John, who was only thirteen, wrote a poem about the lamb as a gift for Miss Kimball. Roulstone's poem went as follows:

Mary had a little lamb,
Its fleece was white as snow;
And everywhere that Mary went,
The lamb was sure to go.

He followed her to school one day;
That was against the rule.
It made the children laugh and play
To see the lamb at school.

And so the teacher turned him out,
But still he lingered near
And waited patiently about
Till Mary did appear.

The years flew by and Miss Kimball's Christmas poem remained buried beneath a pile of papers in her desk drawer. In time, she married and moved away. But the poem remained in the desk at Redstone School.

In 1830, Mrs. Sarah Josepha Hale, editor of *Godey's Magazine for Ladies,* revealed to her subscribers that she was busy at work on a book of poems. She requested readers to submit poems to her. One arrived from Mary's hometown of Sterling. It was from the teacher who had replaced Miss Kimball.

"My offering is about a child and a lamb," wrote the teacher. "I do not claim authorship. I found the dear poem in a desk drawer when I first arrived at the school where I now teach. Please use it as you see fit, if indeed you see fit to use it."

Sarah Hale decided the poem needed some additional verses to give it a moral. She added the following three verses:

And then he ran to her and laid
His head upon her arm,
As if he said, "I'm not afraid.
You'll keep me from all harm."

"What makes the lamb love Mary so?"
The eager children cry.
"Oh, Mary loves the lamb, you know,"
The teacher did reply.

"And you each gentle animal
In confidence may bind,
And make them follow at your call,
If you are always kind."

Parents of long ago recited that little verse to their children when the book was first published. Parents of today do the same.

In December 1888, the editor of a Boston newspaper received a letter from a woman in nearby Somerville. Her name was Mary Sawyer.

"Christmas is near," she wrote, "and I am in my eighties. There may never be another Christmas for me. Do you mind if I take pen in hand and tell you of a Christmas poem written many, many years ago?"

And so the history of the poem came to be known.

When Mary's lamb died about a year after its stroll to Redstone Schoolhouse, Mary's mother knitted two pairs of stockings for her from the fleece sheared off the lamb.

In 1882, Mary unravelled the stockings and tied pieces of the yarn to cards that read: "Knitted from the fleece of Mary's little lamb." She sold these souvenir cards to collectors to help raise money for the preservation of Old South Church in Boston.

Shortly after writing the letter to the newspaper, Mary Sawyer died and was buried in Mt. Auburn Cemetery in Cambridge, Massachusetts. A souvenir card with a piece of Snow's fleece was buried with her.

Dick O'Donnell

A Glimpse of Heaven

When I see the woodland flaming
In a brilliant red and gold;
I can only stand and marvel
At the splendor I behold.

Only could the Master Painter
Clothe a tree in such array;
Seems I get a glimpse of heaven
Every sunny autumn day.

Daniel D. Rodes

Cathedrals of the Forest

Through cathedrals of the forest,
I walk at summer's end.
The elm, the oak, the chestnut—
Oh, how their colors blend!

Like torches flaming, blazing,
They reach to touch the sky;
And in that wooded chapel
I feel my God so nigh.

I hear a scared hush, hush,
As soft winds gently blow
Among the leafy parchments.
With thoughtful steps and slow,

I walk in keen observance
Of summer's vibrant end,
'Midst cathedrals of the forest
As autumn's colors blend.

Georgia B. Adams

Photo Opposite
SKYLINE DRIVE
Jeff Gnass

Call of Freedom

Across the cloudless sky
A winged V-wedge appears;
The wild honk of the goose
Brings thoughts of winter near.

The wild call of freedom
Reaches us far below
And stirs in our hearts the longing
For the freedom wild geese know.

Lois Groover

Night Song

Last night I heard the wild geese fly;
They sounded far away.
And yet I see the countryside
Is turning bronze today.

The sunrise wears a wispy veil
Of Indian Summer smoke;
And on brown hills the cattle graze
Beneath the speckled oak.

I never knew when summer left;
Her exit was so calm.
She must have told the wild geese, though;
Last night I heard their psalm.

June Masters Bacher

Photo Overleaf, CANOPY OF GOLD, Jack Zehrt

Autumn's Wonderland

Jack Frost's dancing 'midst the trees
With paintbrush clutched in hand . . .
Deftly touching up the leaves
In autumn's wonderland.

Splashing gold upon them,
And a dash of crimson red,
As they slowly tumble to the ground
To rest upon their grassy bed.

Rows of golden pumpkins
And shimmering wheat that stands
To await the day of harvest
In autumn's wonderland.

The mums along the cobblestone path,
The bittersweet orange and red,
The strawflowers in the garden
Seem to bow their weary heads.

The honk of wild geese flying
Together in their band . . .
And the golden moon is hanging low
In autumn's wonderland.

Ruth H. Underhill

Autumn Dancers

The dancers on the water are
Bright colored leaves of fall
That float from trees which grace the shore
To join the festive ball.

The orchestra—a cricket's call,
A softly whispering breeze,
The cry of geese in southern flight,
The dove's deep tones of ease.

The dance—a jolly, spritely step
With sunbeams all about,
With dancers bowing gracefully
To partners they've sought out.

The mood is one of peacefulness,
Of idling leaves of fall
That, drifting gently on the breeze,
Bring harmony to all.

Craig E. Sathoff

Photo Opposite
PICTURESQUE COPPER FALLS
Ken Dequaine

Autumn's Extravaganza

The hillside waits, indeed, it calls,
For me to see its extravaganza for fall!
The stage is set, the cast is ready
In brilliant costumes, gay and pretty.

Kneeling on a cushion of fallen leaves,
I wait for the drama, sure to please,
A woodsy aroma is wafted on high
By a breeze, hoping the curtain of fog will rise.

From out of the haze an aspen of gold
Stands quivering and tall for me to behold,
While maples and sumacs with their crimson flare
Thrill and excite me to applaud and stare.

Under the direction of a gentle wind,
Amber leaves trip in and their frolic begins.
Drifting and tumbling, light as a feather,
With rhythm and grace, without care or fetter.

Then as a finale, the sunshine bathes all
In a brightness that endears me to picturesque fall;
That climaxes autumn's extravagant show,
And leaves the hill reveling in its golden glow!

Joy Belle Burgess

AUTUMN WOODS

Let in through all the trees
Come the strange rays; the forest depths are bright;
Their sunny colored foliage, in the breeze,
Twinkles, like beams of light.

The rivulet, late unseen,
Where bickering through the shrubs its waters run,
Shines with the image of its golden screen,
And glimmerings of the sun.

But 'neath yon crimson tree,
Lover to listening maid might breathe his flame
Nor mark, within its roseate canopy,
Her blush of maiden shame.

Oh, Autumn! why so soon
Depart the hues that make thy forests glad,
Thy gentle wind and thy fair sunny noon,
And leave thee wild and sad!

Ah! 'twere a lot too blest
Forever in thy colored shades to stray;
Amid the kisses of the soft southwest
To roam and dream for aye;

And leave the vain low strife
That makes men mad—the tug for wealth and power—
The passions and the cares that wither life,
And waste its little hour.

William Cullen Bryant

Photo Opposite
SOUTH KIRBY, VERMONT
Gene Ahrens

With Eagerness I Walk

With eagerness I walk along
   Among the fallen leaves.
They crunch and rustle 'neath my tread;
   My roaming heart receives

Such pleasure on October days
   When skies above are clear.
When mountainsides are splashed with hues,
   I fill my cup with cheer!

I love the golds, the russets and
   The flaming red of hills.
So much of beauty waits for me;
   There is no end to thrills.

The Indian Summer brings the warmth
   Of summer days now past;
With eagerness I walk along,
   The beauty unsurpassed.

Georgia B. Adams

Wanderlust

A wanderlust may lead one
Beside an ocean shore,
Where waves dash high, then drop low
With a fascinating roar.

Autumn tends to bring this longing,
This thing called wanderlust
For lakes or seas or woodlands;
They seem to be a must.

Wanderlust is captivating
And contagious as disease;
For when you go out walking,
You catch it on the breeze.

Adelaide Blanton

Celebrate Thanksgiving with *Ideals!*

In the next issue of *Ideals*, we celebrate the glory of Thanksgiving. We hope you will share the richness of late autumn, the traditions of the holiday, and the beginning of winter through the beautiful photography and inspirational poetry and prose we have selected for the Thanksgiving issue.

At Ideals, we are thankful for our readers and subscribers who continue to send us letters, ideas, and suggestions. One reader, Ms. Contance Auger of Worcester, Massachusetts, recently shared her opinion of *Ideals* with us:

> *Let me take this opportunity to tell you that I enjoy reading* Ideals *immensely! It is truly an inspiration to all who read it. May it continue for many years to inspire good thoughts and actions in our lives!*

We thank Ms. Auger and all our friends. And we hope that you will join us in our celebration of Thanksgiving. You can also show your thanks for others by giving a subscription to *Ideals*, beginning with our Thanksgiving issue.

ACKNOWLEDGMENTS

Our sincere thanks to the following whose addresses we were unable to locate: Adelaide Blanton for WANDERLUST; Mary Lee Butts for THROUGH A WOODLAND; Inez Franck for RUSTIC PAINTING; Gertrude Holman for BEAUTY IN THE FALL; Bobbe Indgin for HALLOWEEN; Daniel D. Rodes for A GLIMPSE OF HEAVEN.